Whispers of a Parent's Heart

A DEVOTIONAL FOR PARENTS
IN THE
NEONATAL INTENSIVE CARE UNIT

Rev. Elizabeth Hulford, MDiv, BCC

ISBN-13: 978-0615634104
ISBN-10: 0615634109

3RevsLibrary
Oak Forest, IL

Contents

Whispers of a Parent's Heart

Introduction

WHISPERS OF A PARENT'S HEART is a devotional guide written for parents of babies who have to stay in the Neonatal Intensive Care Unit (NICU). Your child may have to stay only a short time or have a long stay with us in the NICU. This devotional attempts to address many common situations parents encounter at their children's bedside.

Not every situation or emotion you will experience in the NICU will be addressed, and hopefully your child will not experience all the scenarios in this booklet. But my hope is that when you are at your baby's bedside, you will be able to open this devotional, find an issue that you are experiencing, see a reflection of yourself in these words, and be able to pray along with them.

This devotional is written in Christian language, but I encourage you, if you are not a Christian, to continue to read this material and pray along with the sentiments according to your own spirituality or religious tradition. This book is not meant to be exclusionary, but to assist in naming your feelings and normalizing them. As well, my hope is that this devotional will inspire you talk about your feelings with your family, friends, and staff. Our NICU is filled with compassionate people who want the best for you and your child, and if you desire, are willing to pray with you when you need it.

Before you begin this journey please note that I find the terminology "he or she" or "he/she" to be awkward. Traditionally, authors have avoided this awkwardness by using masculine pronouns exclusively. I believe this practice perpetuates gender bias. I have chosen instead to alternate the masculine and feminine pronouns throughout this book. I hope this book will be equally useful for parents of daughters and parents of sons.

Whispers of a Parent's Heart

You may have been blessed to be the parent of multiple children; twins, triplets, even quadruplets. This book is written in the language of singletons, but feel free to apply the reflections to each of your children—as individuals or as a collective.

Interspersed with the devotional material are meaningful quotations from various authors on parenthood and children meant to expand on the mystery of parenthood and help empower you for the journey of parenthood.

May you be blessed by reading this devotional.

REV. CHAPLAIN LIZ HULFORD, MDIV, BCC

Prematurity

My baby was born premature

Reflection

YOUR BABY CAME INTO the world a little or a lot early and it can be very hard on him and on you as a parent. Most parents dream of having their baby born perfectly healthy, on their due date, and with no complications whatsoever. Your child decided to reject your birth plan. He came early and has complicated your experience of parenthood from day one. Your vision of parenthood has to be changed not only for your time in the NICU but also perhaps for your son's growing up. You may have to make difficult choices along the way.

Each premature baby is different and follows a different path. You will experience a lot of emotional ups and downs. Tears are normal and natural, they are a sign of how much you love your child and how much hope you have for him. Don't be afraid to cry at your child's bedside, letting those emotions out will only help you be the best parent you can be. Some days your child may excel far beyond imagination, hitting developmental milestones like a champion; and other days it may be difficult to be present with your child due to setbacks and medical procedures.

All of our nurses, doctors, chaplains, and staff are here to support you; you are never alone. Many premature babies grow to be healthy, smart, happy, and well-adjusted kids. But you need not worry about that in this moment. For now, you are being asked to be present and love your little one whether or not you have the opportunity to hold him knowing that only hands of compassion are touching your baby.

Whispers of a Parent's Heart

Prayer

O EVER PRESENT GOD, I am told that you are a great and mighty God and that nothing and no one is too small for you, so I ask that you draw near to my baby. Help him to grow healthy and strong. May he not be overwhelmed by the large world around him. May I as a parent not be overwhelmed by taking care of and loving on someone so small and precious. Give me strength to be by his bedside. Give his doctors wisdom to care for him. Allow my love to reach even the smallest places within him. In the whisper of my heart, I pray. Amen.

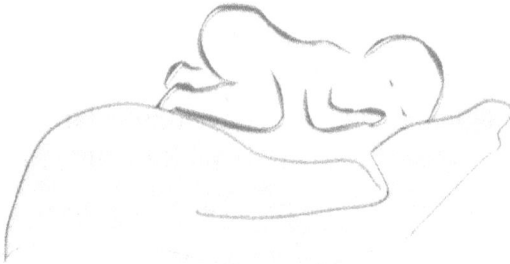

On Children

Your children are not your children.
They are the sons and daughters of Life's longing for itself.
They come through you but not from you,
And though they are with you yet they belong not to you.
You may give them your love but not your thoughts,
For they have their own thoughts.
You may house their bodies but not their souls,
For their souls dwell in the house of tomorrow,
which you cannot visit, not even in your dreams.
You may strive to be like them,
but seek not to make them like you.
For life goes not backward nor tarries with yesterday.
You are the bows from which your children
as living arrows are sent forth.
The archer sees the mark upon the path of the infinite,
and He bends you with His might
that His arrows may go swift and far.
Let your bending in the archer's hand be for gladness;
For even as He loves the arrow that flies,
so He loves also the bow that is stable.

~ Kahlil Gibran

Whispers of a Parent's Heart

Leaving My Baby in the NICU

*I am being asked to leave my baby
in the NICU for the first time*

Reflection

T HE TIME HAS COME for you as parent to leave the hospital and you are being asked to leave your baby here in the NICU. This is a scary, hard moment for all parents.

Mom, it may be especially difficult for you because you have carried this child very close to your heart, literally, since conception. You have a connection to this child that supersedes all other connections in your life. Suddenly you have a piece of your DNA outside of yourself in the world. It is surreal that you even have this child. How can you be separated from your daughter?

Dad, you just met this little girl and you love her already. How can you protect her, provide for her, care for her when you're not together? Who knew it would be so painful to walk away from someone you love?

Your head and your heart may have a hard time rationalizing this idea of walking away from your child in the NICU. It may feel like you're abandoning your child, but you're not. You are leaving your baby in the best hands possible so that she may get what she needs to grow and come home with you. Of course, yours are the best hands to care for your child, but in your place, our staff will care for your baby as if she is our own. It is natural to have lots of tears. It is natural to be unable to sleep when you get home. But we encourage you get some rest. We are only a phone call away and no question is too small or insignificant when it comes to your precious child.

Prayer

G OD OF ALL COMFORT, *please guard between myself and my child while we are apart. All I want is to be near to my baby and to know that she is safe. Please wrap your arms of comfort and mercy around my child. May only hands of compassion and grace touch her while we are apart. May she feel my spirit of love abiding with her till we are together again. In your name I pray. Amen.*

"Jesus said, 'Let the little children come to me, and do not hinder them, for the kingdom of heaven belongs to such as these.' "
~ Matthew 19: 14

The Monitor

I can't stop watching the monitor

Reflection

EACH DAY THAT YOU come to the NICU to be with your baby you are giving your baby a great gift. You are giving your child the gift of your time, your presence, and your attention. But are you giving your child all the attention you can?

It is very tempting to sit by your baby's bedside and watch the monitor. After all, the dinging sound it makes almost begs you to pay attention to it. You have also learned through your time in the NICU what all the numbers mean so you understand all that the monitor can tell you. Some parents feel that by watching the monitor they are getting extra insight into their baby, perhaps by watching the monitor they can figure out what precipitates an episode, and that way they can better care for their baby.

Other parents watch the monitor because in truth, their child isn't doing much. The monitor may be a distraction for you. Whatever reason you watch the monitor, please know that staff is aware of all that the monitor does as well, and if something were truly happening they would be immediately by your baby's bedside.

Watching the monitor can never give you one more second with your child and you, watching the monitor, cannot control what your baby will do. No one has prevented anything from happening to their baby by watching the monitor. In fact, watching your child may be more helpful for staff then watching the monitor ever could be. So please, don't waste your precious time together with your child by watching the monitor.

Prayer

GOD OF ALL POWER, *I thank you for this day and this opportunity to be here with my child. This time is so precious and each day I give thanks for being given the gift of watching my son grow and develop more and more into the boy you have called him to be. In my times of distraction, Lord, please focus my spirit on what truly matters, my son. Bless him, cover him with peace and mercy. Give me the presence to be present in this time. In your name. Amen.*

"We never know the love of a parent, till we become a parent ourselves."

~Henry Ward Beecher

Oxygen

My baby is on oxygen

Reflection

NICU BABIES OFTEN NEED help with the most basic functions of life, things that we take for granted each day, like breathing. Some babies need the help of a ventilator to breathe, or vapotherm, or a nasal cannula.

It can be disconcerting for a parent to see the tube taped to their baby's face. You know intrinsically that the tube doesn't hurt them, but it looks awkward and distracts from the beauty of their face. Furthermore, if you've ever had oxygen given to you as an adult you know it's more uncomfortable and cold than anything else. So as a parent you worry about your baby's ability to breathe.

How long your baby needs oxygen depends on their condition; some babies go back and forth on their oxygen levels, which can be disconcerting; others quickly move off of oxygen; still others end up needing to go home on oxygen. However long your baby might need oxygen and whatever the level may be, your baby's need for oxygen is a sign of the struggle for life, and that oxygen we give your child is simply a way of supporting your child till they are in the best place they can be to come home with you.

Whispers of a Parent's Heart

Prayer

G OD OF ALL BREATH, help my baby to breathe. In this moment I breathe in your spirit to my lungs, and envision your holy breath entering my daughter's lungs. Breathe into my baby's lungs the spirit of healing and love. Let her exhale all toxins and things that might harm her. Let me exhale all worry and concern for her, letting go of my anxiety. Let us be one at peace. Be our rhythmic breath O God and renew our spirits for the living of this day. Amen.

"A mother's love for her child is like nothing else in the world. It knows no law, no pity, it dares all things and crushes down remorselessly all that stands in its path."

~ Agatha Christie

Feeding

My baby is a poor feeder

Reflection

A T SOME POINT IN your NICU stay you may hear the phrase "poor feeder" directed at your child. What this means is that your baby is not eating as well as she should for her age. For some babies this is a simple matter of learning how to suck and swallow at the right time, for others it can be due to a physiological reason.

Either way, it can be disheartening to hear that phrase pointed at your child. And it can be frustrating when your baby won't latch during breastfeeding nor take a bottle as well as she should. The frustration comes from knowing this is something your baby should be able to do but simply can't or won't. Your child is not trying to aggravate you on purpose, nor is she trying to create emotional distance, though it may feel like you or she has failed.

Being a "poor feeder" is not a mark on her permanent record there is always help out there for her and for you. Ask to see a speech therapist or a lactation consultant if her feeding issues get too overwhelming for you. You want the best for your baby, you want her to excel at everything, but sometimes you and she need to have patience in order to become experts at feeding.

Whispers of a Parent's Heart

Prayer

GOD OF ALL SUSTENANCE, thank you for giving us all that we need in this life. Sometimes in the struggle to survive we need help. I pray for patience during this trial of feeding. May I be calm and hopeful for my child. May she be provided with what she needs, if not from me then from someone else. May she improve each day at feeding. Give her what she needs to coordinate her body's functions so that her times of feeding may go smoothly and efficiently. And help us to have patience and grace in those difficult moments. All this I ask, in the name of the one who is a rock in the storm. Amen.

O Lord, you made all the delicate, inner parts of my body and knit me
together in my mother's womb.
Thank you for making me so wonderfully complex!
Your workmanship is marvelous—how well I know it. You watched me as I
was being formed in utter seclusion,
as I was woven together in the dark of the womb.
You saw me before I was born. Every day of my life was recorded in your
book. Every moment was laid out before a single day had passed.
How precious are your thoughts about me, O God.
They cannot be numbered! I can't even count them;
they outnumber the grains of sand!
And when I wake up,
you are still with me!

~ Psalm 139: 13-18

Holding My Baby

I can't hold my baby.

Reflection

A FTER SIX OR MORE months within a mother's womb, a bond between parent and child begins to form. Some parents look to their due date with overflowing joy at the thought of meeting their child. Some parents look to their due date with dread and nervousness about the realities of labor and the ultimate life changing responsibilities ahead. Either way, once a child is born most mothers and fathers feel a deep longing for their children. For some mothers it is overwhelming not to have that physical connection with their child anymore. Depending on your child's situation, she may be hooked up to many machines and cords, which prevent you from holding your child.

Have you asked if you can hold your baby? Don't assume that it cannot be arranged, sometimes the nurses may be able to accommodate you. If not, try to do this meditative exercise. Look at your child, study her. Now close your eyes and take a deep breath in and out. Imagine your muscles lifting your arms up as you carefully draw your baby into your arms. Feel her small frame in your arms, perhaps she fits in just your hand. But feel her warm soft skin. Hold her there. Take a deep breath. Breathe her in. Feel her soft skin. Whisper to her words of comfort and love in your mind's eye. Then set her down again. You can keep repeating this exercise as a way of sending positive love and energy to your child. As well, through this exercise your brain begins to relax and reinforces intimacy between yourself and your child.

Prayer

G OD OF THE SPACES in between, I pray that you occupy the physical space between myself and my child. Fill up that space so that she may know how much I love her. Give my arms and heart comfort and peace as I miss her closeness to me. As I miss her touch, guard between us Lord God so that she may know my love. Amen.

"Can a woman forget her nursing child, or show no compassion for the child of her womb? Even these may forget, yet I, the Lord your God, will not forget you. See, I have inscribed you on the palm of my hands; your walls are ever before me."

~ Isaiah 49: 15-16

Jaundice

My baby has jaundice

Reflection

THE DOCTOR CAME TO you and said "your baby has jaundice." She stood there like she was telling you that the sky is blue, so natural, so obvious. Yet, while she spoke you didn't hear a word she said because all you could think was, "There's something wrong with my baby." You manage to pop back into reality when the doctor says, "We are going to have to put him under the lights." What do those words even mean? Panic sets in, what's going on? Now it's time to take a deep breath.

Jaundice is an elevation of bilirubin levels in your baby's liver. Bilirubin is produced by the breakdown of red blood cells and normally the body processes bilirubin quickly and efficiently, but for some reason your baby's liver has slowed down the breakdown of those cells so it builds up and causes jaundice. Your sweet baby may look a little yellow in his skin or in the whites of his eyes. Almost all babies get some form of jaundice and doctors are careful enough to catch it quickly so it doesn't develop into a problem. Although catching it so quickly might cause you excess anxiety.

Jaundice is treated by keeping your baby under phototherapy where special lights make it easier to process bilirubin. This treatment doesn't hurt your boy, and hopefully it won't take very long a few hours to a few days. Even if your baby has to spend some time under the bili lights, he's safe, the treatment won't hurt him, he's not too hot or uncomfortable, and he's going to emerge healthier than before. You are not alone in this and it's okay to have lots of tears if you hear the word jaundice directed at your child. After all, he's always your baby!

Prayer

GOD WHO UNIFIES ALL colors, thank you for this perfect baby. I know you knit him together perfectly in my womb and that this condition of jaundice will pass but I confess I am afraid for him, for me, for any sort of separation. Please heal my child Lord. Make him whole and perfect in every sense of the word. Bless me as I wait for his return. Bless the hands that care for him to touch him with compassion and love. Help him to feel my love. Bless and heal my baby boy. Amen.

"Through the blur, I wondered if I was alone or if other parents felt the same way I did - that everything involving our children was painful in some way. The emotions, whether they were joy, sorrow, love or pride, were so deep and sharp that in the end they left you raw, exposed and yes, in pain. The human heart was not designed to beat outside the human body and yet, each child represented just that - a parent's heart bared, beating forever outside its chest."

~ Debra Ginsberg

Surgery

My baby has to have surgery

Reflection

THE TIME HAS COME when a serious intervention must be made into the life and health of your child. Surgery. As an adult that word sounds scary enough because you know that with every surgery there are risks, seen and unforeseen. Now, that scary word is directed towards your small, beautiful, helpless child. Your mind spins and of course the directions it spins to are far-reaching and not necessarily rational. How will he survive? How will he handle anesthesia? What if he's not the same afterwards?

Fear is an extremely normal reaction to surgery. Your doctors would not suggest surgery unless it was absolutely necessary. As well, you are putting your child into capable hands and this takes trust, trust that you have been putting forth in our staff since day one.

In many ways, surgery is harder on you, mom and dad, than on your child because he has no idea what's going on or what's coming. You may have postoperative concerns about how well he'll do after surgery. All this makes you as a parent a bundle of nerves. Take a deep breath. Talk out some of your feelings with staff and your family. They may have wisdom from previous experiences that can help allay some of your fears. Remember everyone is hoping for the best for your son! You can handle this!

Prayer

O GREAT COMFORTER, I am in need of comfort in this moment. I am filled with worry, fear, and anxiety about my son facing surgery. Please guide the surgeon's hands to do this surgery with skill, precision, and expertise. Please bless everyone in that operating room to keep my son safe. And bless me as wait and hope for the ability to trust and see my son healthy again. Give me peace of mind to know that you are in control and you are working out something incredibly good for him. With thanksgiving in my heart for the blessing that is my son I pray. Amen.

Children of the Heavenly Father

Children of the heav'nly Father
Safely in His bosom gather;
Nestling bird nor star in Heaven
Such a refuge e'er was given.
God His own doth tend and nourish;
In His holy courts they flourish;
From all evil things He spares them;
In His mighty arms He bears them.
Neither life nor death shall ever
From the Lord His children sever;
Unto them His grace He showeth,
And their sorrows all He knoweth.

Though He giveth or He taketh,
God His children ne'er forsaketh;
His the loving purpose solely
To preserve them pure and holy.
Lo, their very hairs He numbers,
And no daily care encumbers
Them that share His ev'ry blessing
And His help in woes distressing.
Praise the Lord in joyful numbers:
Your Protector never slumbers.
At the will of your Defender
Ev'ry foeman must surrender.

~ Text by Karolina W. Sandell-Berg
translated by Ernst W. Olson

Being Left Behind

My baby's neighbor is going home, but we have to stay.

Reflection

AS YOU SPEND TIME in the NICU you may develop a sense of community with some of the other moms and we encourage that. It is good to discover friendships with other parents and we encourage you to connect outside of the NICU. After all, no one understands what you are going through more than another parent going through similar circumstances. While you form friendships, you begin to hope and grieve together so it's understandable that you might experience some conflicting emotions when your baby's neighbor is preparing to leave for home.

It's not uncommon to be jealous and wonder "why can't my baby leave too? When is our turn?" You may be happy for the neighbor's family but sad for your own. Frustration increases when your hope for your own child rises but does not reach the height you desire. Fear not! There will come a time, the appropriate time, for your child to come home with you. Though it is easy to be discouraged, take heart with the knowledge that your baby is still safe and getting the best care possible. We hope your baby comes home with you soon.

Whispers of a Parent's Heart

Prayer

O GOD OF OUR comings and goings; our time is not in our hands but in yours. I give you thanks that our neighbor gets to head home and may they be blessed in their journey. Forgive my jealousy of their blessings. I pray that we might be able to journey home together soon. In the meantime, bless my daughter with health and happiness, and my heart with the peace of knowing that wherever we go we are in your care. Amen.

"In the midst of the affliction He counsels, strengthens confirms, nourishes, and favors us.... Moreover, when we have repented, He instantly remits the sins as well as the punishments. In the same manner parents ought to handle their children."

~ Martin Luther

Breastfeeding

I can't breastfeed my baby

Reflection

A LOT OF PLANNING goes into having a baby and you may have had a birth plan that included breastfeeding your child immediately after birth and onwards. But due to the early arrival of your child these plans have had to change. So you have to use the pump instead of putting your son to breast.

And let's be honest, pumping is not that enjoyable. In fact, it's more like work because the lactation consultant has told you that you need to pump every three hours even at night. Eight times a day you have to take time out from your busy schedule, sit, attach yourself to a machine, and wait for your milk to come down. IF the milk even comes at all. It's discouraging after a while and doesn't feel as bonding as putting your child to your breast. You miss that connection and closeness that makes breastfeeding seem so worthwhile.

But take heart, don't give up, whatever you can give your son is good. It's a gift that surpasses understanding what breast milk can do for your child. Ask to speak to the lactation consultant for possible aides to help you find more success at pumping or counsel on how to proceed. And take caution, because once you stop it's extremely hard to start up again. Just remember there are no medals given out for success at breastfeeding so there's no shame in stopping when you feel it's time.

Whispers of a Parent's Heart

Prayer

GOD OF ALL SUSTENANCE, I long for my child. I long to give my child the milk that will sustain and nourish his life. But I feel discouraged and downtrodden at the thought of using this pump day in and day out. Encourage me as my spirit weakens Lord. Provide grace to me in my moments of frustration. Be the abiding nourishment for my son when I am not enough. Amen.

O, thou beautiful damsel, may the four oceans
Of the earth contribute the secretion of milk
In thy breasts for the purpose for improving
The bodily strength of the child
O, thou with the beautiful face, may the child
Reared on your milk, attain a long life, like
The gods made immortal with drinks of nectar

~Sushruta Samhita, translated

Sleeping

My baby sleeps all the time; why won't she wake up for me?

Reflection

YOUR BABY IS SO cute! You could look at her and hold her all day but you worry about her sleeping all the time. You can't sleep all the time, why is she doing that? Is she okay? All you really want is to hear her voice and see her eyes. Even to hear her cry would make you feel more of a connection. You want to interact with your child, which is great and healthy.

It is important to realize that babies need lots of sleep, especially premature babies because this is when they grow and develop. It is frustrating that she sleeps while you are able to be at her bedside, as well you might hear reports from the nurses that she was up all night and you missed it. It almost feels like you are being left out of her life. So you touch her, coo to her and adore her but you can't help but wonder; to what end?

All this attention you give her is a great gift. It solidifies the bond between you and your child. She feels your presence and your spirit. Even in her sleep you mean so much to her. By being with her you are being an excellent parent. So let her sleep and delight in the moments when she is awake because those are the extra special times with her.

Whispers of a Parent's Heart

Prayer

O GOD OF ALL comfort, as I long for those moments of interaction and connection with my child I pray for peace in my heart and in hers. May she in her blissful sleep continue to grow healthy and strong. May I, at her bedside, be a comfort to her and may she know that I love her deeply. Amen.

"How soft and fresh he breathes! Look! He is dreaming! Visions sure of joy Are gladdening his rest; and, ah! who knows But waiting angels do converse in sleep With babes like this!"

~ Bishop Arthur Cleveland Coxe (1818-1896)

Going Home

I am taking my baby home.

Reflection

A T THE BIRTH OF your child expectations and hopes are at their highest. You weathered the storms of emotions and situations that arise by having a baby in the NICU. You've wanted to take your baby home since the moment he arrived but through the hospital stay you've grown used to a large staff taking care of your little guy and encouraging you in taking care of him. It seems daunting now to take your child home with you. What does it mean to be a parent? What does it mean to be *his* parent?

It is normal to feel concerned about being ready to care for him. It is important to know that no one really feels "ready" to take their child home, no matter how long their child has been in the hospital. This child was meant for you. He comes from you, he's a part of you and your partner, he is wrapped in your love. You will make mistakes, all parents do, hopefully no grievous ones, but love can forgive all things. At the same time, you've established bonds with staff and feel a sense of loss at the thought of not being around these people who have supported you so much. It is normal to feel grief and hope at the same time. Know that our thoughts and prayers go with you into your parenthood journey. You, your baby, and your family will never be forgotten. You are now free to be the parent that you have been called to be.

Whispers of a Parent's Heart

Prayer

*H*OLY GOD, I'VE BEEN *entrusted with this precious little child. Help me to serve this child well. Give me wisdom for his growth and development. Help me to inspire him and bless him for the living of these days. Give me patience and peace of mind to know when to ask for help and when to trust my son to his own freedom. Help us all to grow in faith, hope, and love. Amen.*

"No one is ever quite ready; everyone is always caught off guard. Parenthood chooses you. And you open your eyes, look at what you've got, say "Oh, my gosh," and recognize that of all the balls there ever were, this is the one you should not drop. It's not a question of choice."

~ Marisa de los Santos, LOVE WALKED IN.

ELIZABETH HULFORD IS A native of Lansdowne, PA. She is a graduate of Calvin College and has a Master of Divinity from Eastern Baptist Theological Seminary. She is a Board Certified Chaplain with the Association of Professional Chaplains and an ordained Presbyterian Pastor. She has worked in the Neonatal Intensive Care Environment for over five years with Adventist Hinsdale Hospital. Currently, Elizabeth resides in the Chicago area with her husband and two beautiful sons.

Whispers of a Parent's Heart

www.ingramcontent.com/pod-product-compliance
Lightning Source LLC
Chambersburg PA
CBHW071449040426
42445CB00012BA/1491